Bodybuilders

small group bible resources

Growing through change

seizing the opportunities
life gives you

Lance Pierson

Scripture Union, 207–209 Queensway, Bletchley, MK2 2EB, England.
Email:info@scriptureunion.org.uk
www.scriptureunion.org.uk

Scripture Union Australia, Locked Bag 2, Central Coast Business Centre, NSW 2252

Small Group Resources, 1 Hilton Place, Harehills, Leeds, LS8 4HE

Main text © Small Group Resources, 2002.
Additional icebreakers, prayer and worship ideas © Scripture Union, 2002.

Note: *Growing Through Change* was originally published under the title *Must Get Changed*.

ISBN 1 85999 583 7

All rights reserved. The activity sheets and illustrations in this book may be photocopied for use in Christian ministry. This permission is granted freely to owners of this book. This arrangement does not allow the printing of any of the published material in permanent form. Nor does it allow the printing of words or illustrations for resale or for any commercial use. Apart from this, no part of this publication may be reproduced, stored in a retrieval system, or transmitted, in any form or by any means, electronic, mechanical, photocopying, recording or otherwise, without the prior permission of Small Group Resources.

The right of Lance Pierson to be identified as author of this work has been asserted by him in accordance with the Copyright, Designs and Patents Act 1988.

Scripture quotations are taken from the Holy Bible, New International Version. Copyright © 1973, 1978, 1984 by International Bible Society. Anglicisation copyright © 1979, 1984, 1989. Used by permission of Hodder and Stoughton Ltd.

British Library Cataloguing-in-Publication Data
A catalogue record for this book is available from the British Library.

Cover design by David Lund Design
Internal page design by David Lund Design
Internal page layout by Mac Style Ltd, Scarborough, N. Yorkshire

Printed and bound in Great Britain by Ebenezer Baylis & Son Ltd, The Trinity Press, London Road, Worcester WR5 2JH

Introducing Bodybuilders

 **ORIGINS AND APPROACH**

BODYBUILDERS resources have a strong emphasis on building relationships, helping groups discover the real meaning of **koinonia** – the loving fellowship of Christian believers within which people really care for one another. Group members are encouraged to apply God's Word in ways that produce action and change – all within a secure, supportive atmosphere.

This relational approach to small group experience was first developed in the US by author Lyman Coleman under the title *Serendipity*. In the 1980s Scripture Union, in partnership with another publisher, *Small Group Resources*, took that as the foundation of nine studies under the *Serendipity* branding specially written for the UK market.

This **BODYBUILDERS** series recognises the value and strength of the *Serendipity* approach and contains much of the original material. In a sense, homegroups of the early 21st century may be far more ready to adopt this relational approach than their predecessors. Home groups have moved on; expectations have changed. Revisions and extra new material reflect that progress and also make the series pioneering in the sense of providing a more complete off-the-shelf package.

Christians are not immune from the pressures of society – stresses in the home, workplace, college, places of social interaction. When questioned, most people admit to a deep need for security, a sense of belonging, and a safe environment in which to share themselves and be given support. Many are dissatisfied with the superficial relationships that often characterise contemporary living. They identify lonely chasms in their inner beings, empty of meaningful relationships. They long for practical ways in which to work out their heart commitment to Jesus Christ.

Central to the approach is an understanding that satisfying relationships can be nurtured in small groups in dynamic ways when people are prepared to take risks in opening themselves up to God and to each other. This shared vulnerability works within four contexts:

- **storytelling**
- **affirmation**
- **goal setting**
- **koinonia**

People need to share themselves and need to hear others sharing their own lives for relationships to grow. This is **storytelling**. Everyone needs to be listened to. When we respond to someone with a 'thank you', or 'I found your contribution helpful', we demonstrate that they are valuable and have a contribution to make to the growth of others. This is **affirmation**. Experiencing this in a group that meets regularly – even over a limited time – people begin to share their deeper longings or hurts, discovering that they can trust others for support in their struggles. Individuals can listen for what God is saying to them and implement

True security

changes – **goal setting** within the security of **koinonia**. **BODYBUILDERS** encourage all these stages to be reached through Bible study.

MEETING NEEDS IN CHURCHES AND COMMUNITIES

BODYBUILDERS aim to meet:

- **the need for applied biblical knowledge** – Christians are crying out for help in applying their faith in a confusingly complex world. Knowing what the Bible says isn't enough; people want to know how to translate knowledge into action.
- **the need to belong** – increasing pressures, accelerating pace of life, constant change: these work against committed relationships, which many feel should be a distinctive feature of the local church as it witnesses to a lonely generation.
- **the need to share the burden** – pressures on Christians are often intolerable, as demonstrated by emotional/ psychological disorders, increasing divorce rates, and the problems of ineffective parenting. One answer is for Christians to take seriously the sharing of each others' burdens – not only prayerfully but practically.
- **the need to build the church as community** – there is a growing conviction that the church should be a community living out the true nature of God's kingdom, experiencing New Testament koinonia.

BODYBUILDERS IN PRACTICE

Using BODYBUILDERS to form new groups: The ideal size for a group is between five and 12, meeting in a home or a church. Newcomers can be added into the group at any time, but care should be taken to give them a thorough briefing on 'the story so far'. The particular purposes of the group in growing relationships and discovering how to apply Bible truths to everyday life need to be made plain.

Using BODYBUILDERS in established groups: This material differs from much on the market to resource small groups. Make sure from the outset that the group appreciates that it is more interactive and, in some ways, more demanding. There is an emphasis on application as well as understanding.

Leading the BODYBUILDERS Group: If belonging to this group can be demanding, leading it is more so! The leader needs to have thought about the **BODYBUILDERS** approach and the goals. Ideally, there needs to be knowledge of the group, too, so that the material can be adapted to meet their particular needs. Options are given, and it is the leader who decides which and how much of that material is appropriate. Bearing in mind the emphasis on relationship building, the leader must ensure the group does not become a 'clique', too inward-looking or isolated. The leader makes sure everyone has a chance to speak, assisting those who find contributing difficult. He or she may need to take the initiative in promoting relationship building, which might include practical things like providing lists of telephone numbers, encouraging lift sharing, even organising a baby-sitting rota, as well as exercising pastoral care and leadership.

Each group member needs to feel committed to building relationships and willing to share personally. Regular attendance is a priority. Members aim to make themselves available to each other. Make sure everyone knows that there is complete confidentiality in respect of all

intro

that is shared. Encourage prayer for each other between meetings – and set an example yourself.

Practically speaking, you will need plenty of pens and large sheets of plain paper, and sometimes supplies of felt-tip pens, scissors, glue and old magazines or newspapers. Some Icebreakers need pre-prepared visual aids, or even some re-arrangement of furniture! Look ahead to plan for the coming sessions.

All the booklets in this series, each self-contained, contain material for six sessions. Some groups may want to add an introductory evening to explain the **BODYBUILDERS** approach, perhaps in a social setting over a pot-luck meal. The material can be worked through at a slower pace, if that is preferred.

Most of the interactive material is confined to a double-page spread for each session, so that the leader can photocopy it as an A4 sheet to be given out. Alternatively, everyone can have their own copy of the book. Make sure you allow people enough time to jot down answers on their response sheets. Ring the changes: sometimes it's helpful for people to complete responses in twos or threes, especially when a little discussion time is appropriate.

Variety and freedom are hallmarks of the **BODYBUILDERS** material. Leaders can select from the material to put together each session's programme:

Prayer/ Worship (variable time) – options are given, so that you can tailor your selection to whatever your group feels most comfortable with. Hymns and songs suggested are drawn from several popular collections currently on the market published by Kingsway: various editions *of Songs and Hymns of Fellowship, Spring Harvest Praise, New Songs* and *Stoneleigh* and *The Source*. Your group may be more comfortable with songs from other traditions. It is always helpful, though, to try to match songs to the theme.

Icebreaker (15 minutes) – this warm-up session is intended to relax the group and focus them on being together, and is usually based on the theme.

Relational Bible study (15 minutes) – this is an initial, fairly light excursion into the Bible verses, relating them to the lives of those in the group through multiple choice questions. If the group is large or time is limited, it may be that not everyone shares every question. By the way, Bible verses quoted in **BODYBUILDERS** almost always come from the NIV (New International Version), but you can use another translation. Often it's helpful to have a selection of different translations to compare when studying a particular passage.

In Depth (20 minutes) – moving deeper into the Bible verses, discovering more about their relationship to life.

My story (10–20 minutes) – an encouragement for people to relate teaching to everyday lives.

Going further (15 minutes) – this often involves other parts of the Bible containing similar teaching. If not used during group time, this can be taken away for further personal study during the week.

Enjoy! Discover! Grow!

IN THE SAME SERIES ...

BODYBUILDERS
small group Bible resources

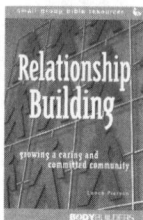

Relationship Building – growing a caring and committed community
Lance Pierson

It's impossible to live daily life without constant interaction with the people around us: family, neighbours, friends or workmates. These six sessions will help you and your group develop the skills needed to build healthy relationships.
ISBN 1 85999 582 9

Designed for great things – wrestling with human nature
Anton Baumohl

Human beings – beautiful and unique yet rebellious and capable of evil! Only the Christian view of man makes real sense of the good and bad things about being human. These six sessions will help you and your group to discover your true potential in Christ.
ISBN 1 85999 585 3

Living for the King – growing God's rule in our world
'Tricia Williams

'God in control? It doesn't look like it!' Is that your reaction to the suffering and injustice you see in the world? These six sessions look at key issues which have immediate relevance for those who want to be involved in the risky and exciting business of being God's community here and now.
ISBN 1 85999 584 5

Surviving under pressure – finding strength in the tough times
Christopher Griffiths & Stephen Hathway

We live in high-pressure days, bombarded with conflicting views and influences that can be obstacles to adopting lifestyles that truly reflect Christian values and principles. These six sessions are aimed at equipping Christian believers to stand firm even on the roughest ground.
ISBN 1 85999 585 X

A Fresh Encounter – meeting the real Jesus
David Bolster

Some were intrigued, attracted to him, accepted, loved and followed him; others were afraid of him, were disturbed by him or rejected him. These six sessions challenge you and your group to extend your understanding of who Jesus is and what that means in everyday life.
ISBN 1 85999 586 1

Available from all good Christian bookshops or from Scripture Union Mail Order:
PO Box 5148, Milton Keynes MLO, MK2 2YX, Tel: 01908 856006
or online through www.scriptureunion.org.uk

GROWING THROUGH CHANGE
– seizing the opportunities life gives you

INTRO

Put not your trust in princes,
  in a son of man, in whom there is no help.
When his breath departs he returns to his earth;
  on that very day his plans perish.
Happy is he whose help is the God of Jacob,
  whose hope is the Lord his God,
  who made heaven and earth,
  the sea and all that is in them;
  who keeps faith for ever;
  who executes justice for the oppressed;
  who gives food to the hungry.
The Lord sets the prisoners free;
  the Lord opens the eyes of the blind.
The Lord lifts up those who are bowed down;
  the Lord loves the righteous.
The Lord watches over the sojourners,
  he upholds the widow and the fatherless;
  but the way of the wicked he brings to ruin.
The Lord will reign for ever,
  thy God, O Zion, to all generations.
Praise the Lord!

Psalm 146:3-10 RSV

Many Christians think that 'change' is almost a dirty word! They assume that change will be for the worse. The prospect of change is frequently a source of anxiety.

Yet as believers we are called to *grow in the grace and knowledge of our Lord and Saviour Jesus Christ* (2 Peter 3:18). There is no growth without change. The danger in resisting all change on principle is that we may get stuck and stop growing – spiritually as well as in other areas of our lives.

One reason why some Christians fear change is that we put our emotional security in things or people – which may include our church, the form of worship our church has adopted, even a fellowship group – and rely on them to stay constant. But God keeps trying to wean us from our dependence on frail substitutes, and on to himself – the only true security. He uses the turbulent and demanding changes of life to invite us to find refuge and peace in him. As one wise saying puts it, 'Change is the angel of the changeless God'; we should positively welcome it!

While, as we have said, we should not find our security in other Christians, it is true that God gives them to us as a support during the pain and upheaval of change. These **BODYBUILDER** studies aim to help us grow and move forward as Christian people; at the same time they seek to encourage the development of a warm and caring support group. In such a setting we can grow the courage we need to face and implement change.

1 Growing through change

CHANGE FOR THE BETTER

AIM: to see Christian discipleship as a process of change and growth in which our developing values and attitudes control the way we behave.

NOTES FOR LEADERS
It will be important to establish an atmosphere of warmth and trust in which people are encouraged to contribute and know that they will be valued for any contribution they make. Spend a few minutes giving an overview of the subjects to be covered, and make sure that everyone knows the number of meetings and venues.

PRAYER/WORSHIP IDEAS

Opening prayer
Try to gather together all the group's anticipation, excitement and maybe even apprehension at the prospect of the next few weeks – not just the subject matter under discussion but also the relationship building that will be happening.

Worship
As this is a first meeting for the group, encourage members to be free to express themselves in worship in ways they find meaningful, and to be accepting of the way others may choose to worship. Make clear that clapping or raising hand or arms etc are acceptable (indeed, biblical!), as are different postures for prayer (kneeling, sitting, standing etc).

Throughout the six meetings it would be helpful to choose hymns or songs which focus on the dependability and constancy of God as well as those which reflect truths particularly relevant to the weekly studies. For this opening meeting some suggestions are:

A new commandment
Change my heart, O God
Have thine own way, Lord
I am a new creation
Jesus, take me as I am
Lord, I come to you, let my heart be changed, renewed
Take my life, and let it be

During the meeting
Give everyone an A4 sheet of paper on which to draw the outline of a range of mountains. Invite them to label each one briefly with an area of change, difficulty or struggle in their family life. Encourage them to include things like 'anxiety about Dan's possible redundancy', 'Julie's truancy', 'Jim's struggle with his mortgage payments', 'Mel's breast lump/waiting for biopsy results'. Choose one to pray about with a partner.

Closing prayer
Pick up on anything that has come out during discussion, particularly in the My Story slot.

ICEBREAKER
How much has everyone changed in the last ten years? (If the group is mostly young, you may want to shorten the backward look to five years.) On the back of their 'mountain range' sheet, everyone should draw a cross creating four areas, labelling them 'work/education', 'family', 'physical/health' and 'spiritual'. Write in each square one way in which you have changed over the past ten years. Then put a plus sign in every square where the change has been for the better, a minus sign where the change has been for the worse, and an equals sign where the change has been neutral. Discuss your 'change charts' in twos or threes.

BIBLE READING
Ephesians 4:17-32

leader's notes

RELATIONAL BIBLE STUDY
Help people in discussion, if it's needed, to see that the fundamental change required by Christian discipleship is in *the attitude of your minds* (4:23). Moral behaviour, music taste, etc may or may not have appeared to have changed radically; the important thing is for people to be under the control of a mind submitted to Christ.

IN DEPTH
Ideally, encourage people to share their answers in full. But if the group do not yet know and trust each other well enough, go for a shorter alternative, such as sharing with each other the area of life in which they find it hardest to make progress as a Christian.

MY STORY

GOING FURTHER
If you plan to use Question 3, you need to have thought about suitable leaders in your church who would be available to counsel if needed.

Things to remember ...

notes on the Bible verses

 **Ephesians 4:17-32**

The passage looks at the radical change in values and lifestyle required of someone who becomes a Christian – a clean break from the way the rest of the world lives (4:17-20) and a new self to replace the old way of life (4:22-24).

In this radical transformation, values control lifestyle; the mind controls behaviour.

4:17 *Gentiles:* Paul does not mean all non-Jews; most of his readers were Gentiles in that racial sense. He uses the word with its Old Testament religious associations of 'everyone outside God's covenant people'. The equivalent for us today would be the non-Christian world around us.

4:18,19: Although non-Christians are separated from God by their ignorance and lack of spiritual sensitivity, this is not something 'they can't help'. Their sensuous lifestyle begins with a deliberate hardening of their hearts. God holds people responsible for their basic attitudes as well as their actions.

4:22-24: The tenses of the original Greek are instructive here. *Put off ... put on ...* refer to a past action. When we consciously opted to follow Christ, we gave a once-for-all assent to change our spiritual clothes. But to be made new implies continuous development. We are in a continuous process of having our attitudes renewed by God.

1 Growing through change

CHANGE FOR THE BETTER

BIBLE READING
Ephesians 4:17-32

RELATIONAL BIBLE STUDY

1 Compared with the Gentiles of 4:17-19, my past — before I was a Christian — was (circle the most appropriate letter):

a just as bad.
b even worse.
c quite tame, really.
d less complicated than now.
e can't remember.
f I've always been a Christian.
g other _____

2 Ephesians 4:22-24 pictures Christian growth as a process of changing your clothes. Put a cross on the line to mark what stage of the process you feel you are at just now.

OLD SELF corrupted by deceitful desires	BEING MADE NEW in attitude of mind	NEW SELF true righteousness and holiness
old clothes	down to my underwear	new clothes on and looking good!

3 How far has your attitude to each of the following changed (if at all) since your Christian faith came alive? Give yourself 0 for no change, 5 for total transformation!

ambitions   0 1 2 3 4 5
politics   0 1 2 3 4 5
clothes   0 1 2 3 4 5
finances   0 1 2 3 4 5
musical taste   0 1 2 3 4 5
religious beliefs 0 1 2 3 4 5

IN DEPTH

Review each of the areas of life Paul mentions in 4:25-32. How far have you progressed in the direction he talks about? Give yourself a score between 0 and 5: 0 for no progress, 5 for mission accomplished!

1 Speech (v25 and v29) 0 1 2 3 4 5
2 Anger (v26 and v31)   0 1 2 3 4 5
3 Work (v28)   0 1 2 3 4 5
4 Love (v32)   0 1 2 3 4 5

What area of your life is God working on now? (It may be quite different from the four above.)

photocopiable response sheet

MY STORY

1 What is your attitude to change in general? Circle any appropriate letters.

a Over my dead body!
b OK, as long as it's change for the better, not change for change's sake.
c Change does you good occasionally.
d Change is a necessary sign of life and growth.
e Other _____

2 4:24 recommends us to *put on the new self*? What improvement do you think God wants to work on in you this week?

a in your attitudes
_____
_____
_____

b in your family/social life
_____
_____
_____
_____

c in your work/main daytime occupation
_____
_____
_____
_____

d in your relationships to others
_____
_____
_____
_____

Is there one phrase from the Bible verses that you could adopt as a personal challenge for the coming week?

going further

1 When someone comes to know Christ (4:20), what *exactly* changes in them? In what sense are they a *new self* (4:24)? It may help to think of some of the other New Testament images for becoming a Christian – eg conversion, new birth, adoption into God's family, being put right with God.

2 In his booklet *Your mind matters* (IVP 1972), Christian leader John Stott traces several areas of Christian discipleship in which the Bible expects our minds to control our actions. Study some of this teaching yourself.

worship – John 4:24; Luke 10:27; 1 Corinthians 4:13–20
holiness – John 8:32; Philippians 4:8; Colossians 3:1,2; Romans 8:5,6
guidance – Ephesians 5:17; Psalm 32:8,9
evangelism – 2 Corinthians 5:11; Acts 17:2–4, 19:8–10

3 Have you any anger you need to resolve or get rid of (4:26, 27, 31)? If you need help with this, ask one of the leaders of your group or church.

4 Starting with 4:28, summarise the Bible's teaching on work. Look up relevant uses of the words 'work' and 'serve' in a concordance. What contribution could this teaching made to relieving the problem of unemployment?

2 | Growing through change

WIND OF CHANGE

AIM: to identify the Holy Spirit as the source of growth and change in our lives as Christians; to monitor the changes he is making, and to respond positively.

NOTES FOR LEADERS
Allow time at the beginning of the session for feedback for anything from the last session, especially about things that people were planning to put into practice. Sensitivity will be needed to ensure that this isn't threatening to anyone.

The focus for this session is the Holy Spirit as the agent of change and growth in our lives. Some Christians are confused about the role and work of the Holy Spirit. You may need to check people's understanding at different points in the meeting, and you may need to allow for some extra discussion, or you may decide it's appropriate to defer some issues until another time.

PRAYER/ WORSHIP IDEAS

Opening prayer
Spend some time as a group thanking God for sending the Holy Spirit to be a source of power, comfort and guidance to his people.

Songs and hymns
Continue with themes from the first meeting, but also choose some songs and hymns that focus on the Holy Spirit and his work in individuals and in the church. Suggestions include:

Be still, for the presence of the Lord
Breathe on me, breath of God
For I'm building a people of power
Hold me, Lord, in your arms
Let there be love shared among us
Living under the shadow of his wings
O breath of life, come sweeping through us
When the Spirit of the Lord is within my heart
Where the Spirit of the Lord is

During the meeting
In twos or threes recall times when you have particularly experienced the closeness of the Holy Spirit. Together say prayers of thanks.

It may be appropriate to close the My Story section with prayer for the Holy Spirit to meet everyone's deepest needs, either praying for the whole group as leader, or in twos or threes.

Closing prayer
Pray as a group for the Holy Spirit to be at work in your church, passing a lit candle or other small symbolic object around the circle, using a continuous stream of one-sentence prayers for the members and the church activities eg 'Holy Spirit, be at work in the youth group at they spend time together at camp next week', 'Holy Spirit, give inspiration to Dave as he prepares to lead this Sunday's communion service', 'Thank you, Holy Spirit, that you have drawn Lois to believe in Jesus and that she wants to be baptised.'

ICEBREAKER
The Holy Spirit brought the Christian church to life at Pentecost with *a sound like the blowing of a violent wind* (Acts 2:2).
On a flip chart you've prepared in advance, show the group the Beaufort Scale of wind force, used in shipping forecasts:

leader's notes

0	calm
1–3	light breeze
4	moderate breeze
5	fresh breeze
6	strong breeze
7	near gale
8	gale
9	severe gale
10	storm force wind
11	severe storm
12–17	hurricane, with a range of force

Ask the group to discuss, in twos or threes…

a the force of the wind of change you think the disciples experienced on the Day of Pentecost.

b the force of the wind of change you think you experienced when you first encountered the Holy Spirit.

c the force of the wind of change you think you are currently experiencing in your spiritual life.

BIBLE READING
Psalm 51:10-12; Romans 12:2; 2 Corinthians 3:16-18; 4:16

RELATIONAL BIBLE STUDY

IN DEPTH

MY STORY

GOING FURTHER

notes on the Bible verses

**Psalm 51:10-12;
Romans 12:2;
2 Corinthians 3:16-18,
4:16**

Psalm 51 is David's confession, traditionally believed to have followed his adultery with Bathsheba and murder of her husband. Sin makes us feel shut out from God's presence (51:11) and takes away our spiritual joy (51:12). We can be assured of salvation (see John 10:27-29), but we are urged to get right with God quickly and be restored into a loving relationship with him, just as the prodigal son was restored to his father (Luke 15).

The Romans verse takes up the theme of our first session, that Christian growth is fuelled by the continuous process of the Holy Spirit renewing our minds and attitudes. The renewed Christian mind does not fall into the rut of man-centred ideas fashionable in the world around us, but aims to align itself with the way God thinks and sees things. There is no renewal without radical God-centred thinking.

In the 2 Corinthians verses we learn that renewal is growth towards possessing and revealing the glory of Jesus in our lives. Initiating and controlling this process is the Holy Spirit – three times identified by Paul with the Lord Jesus. He sets us free from the *veil* of spiritual blindness, so that we can *see*, understand and adore Jesus' glory.

The outward wasting of the human frame (2 Corinthians 4:16) through ageing, illness, accident or whatever, is not for the Christian the tragedy it seems to those whose horizons are limited to this life. Inner faculties are being developed for future use. Renewal is as needed for the next life as for this one.

2 | Growing through change

WIND OF CHANGE

BIBLE READING
Psalm 51:10-12; Romans 12:2; 2 Corinthians 3:16-18; 4:16

RELATIONAL BIBLE STUDY

1 Which Bible 'picture' of the Holy Spirit best helps you to understand him? (Tick the most appropriate.)

__ wind (Acts 2:2; John 3:8)
__ fire (Luke 3:16,17)
__ water (John 7:37-39)
__ oil (Acts 10:38)
__ dove (John 1:32,33)
__ other _____

2 According to the Bible readings for the meeting, what is spiritual renewal? Tick any appropriate letters and give the verse/verses on which you are basing your answer.

a A once-for-all change on becoming a Christian_____
b A later filling of the Holy Spirit _____
c Receiving charismatic gifts _____
d Daily growth in holiness_____
e Forgiveness after sin _____
f Re-moulding of our attitudes _____
g Other _____

IN DEPTH

1 Try to measure the Holy Spirit's progress in renewing you. Mark a cross on the line between each of the contrasting situations mentioned or implied by our Bible passages which represents where you are now.

Psalm 51
weakness _____steadfastness

spirit unwilling to do God's will _____ a willing spirit

Romans 12
conformed to the world's pattern _____ transformed by a renewed mind

2 Corinthians 3
not like Jesus in his glory _____ like Jesus in his glory

2 This self-examination makes me want to ... (tick any appropriate answers)

a give up.
b run away and hide.
c ask the Holy Spirit for help.
d start all over again.
e praise the Lord for his perseverance.
f rejoice in at least some progress.
g keep going with renewed determination.
h other _____

photocopiable response sheet

MY STORY

1 What pattern of change and growth have you seen in your life as a Christian? Has it been a gradual progression, or a series of ups and downs? Draw a line on the first graph to show the pattern of change in your life. Then on the other graph, draw a line to show the pattern of change that the verses from 2 Corinthians suggest. How do the two graphs compare?

2 Circle those that are true for you. At this point in my life I most need the Holy Spirit to …

a strengthen me not to sin.
b restore the joy of my salvation.
c transform my values/ attitudes.
d teach me God's will.
e set me free.
f make me more like Jesus.
g encourage me not to lose heart.
h other _____

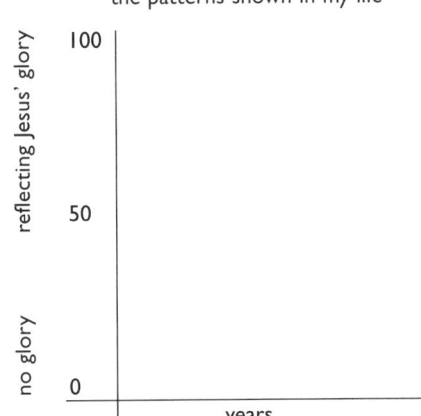

going further

1 The Bible passages for this meeting give virtually the only uses in the Bible of the words *renew/ renewing/ renewed* to describe *spiritual renewal*. The others are Colossians 3:10 (a passage parallel to Ephesians 4:23 which we looked at in Growing Through Change 1) and Titus 3:5. How far does what is conveyed in these verses coincide or clash with the common understanding of *renewal* or the *renewal movement* in the church today?

2 How does joy differ (if at all) from happiness? Use a concordance to gather together the Bible's teaching about joy. Does joy increase as we grow spiritually more mature, or does it 'calm down'?

3 Growing through change

CHANGE OF DIRECTION

AIM: to explore the Holy Spirit's role in guiding our path through life, sometimes in expected directions; to face up to any changes of direction he may be calling us to now; and to give practice in following him.

NOTES FOR LEADERS

PRAYER/ WORSHIP IDEAS

Opening prayer
Pray a prayer of confidence in God using the words of Psalm 46.

Songs and hymns
Include some songs that refer to God's guidance. Interestingly, many that do are hymns from an older era. It's not a subject much taken up by contemporary songwriters. Does postmodern society feel too much in control of its own destiny? Suggestions to look at:

Break thou the bread of life
Father, I place into your hands
Guide me, O thou great Jehovah
I could sing unending songs
I know not why God's wondrous grace
In heavenly love abiding
Master, speak! Thy servant heareth

During the meeting
On sheets of A4 paper, get each person to draw two roads crossing. In each of the four areas created, ask everyone to describe either in words or in a simple cartoon an area where a change of direction might be needed – in their life or the life of someone they know, eg. 'Tim and I have to decide about which school to send Sarah to', 'My line manager has suggested a reworking of my job description', 'Neil and Jennie are starting marriage guidance counselling next week'. Pray silently for all the people involved. Choose one of the four to pray about with a partner.

Closing prayer
Using words from the closing verses of Romans 8 ('If God is for us, who is against us?...) pray for courage to identify and make life-changing decisions, referring as appropriate to some of the situations raised during the meeting.

ICEBREAKER
You will need to prepare in advance a sufficient number of blindfolds and a collection of small items to distribute around the room. Divide into groups of three or four, one of whom should be blindfolded. The blindfolded people should be guided by the spoken directions of the members of their groups (staying in their seats!) to search out and find the objects. Depending on the number of groups and the loudness of the shouting, this may not be as easy as it sounds! When all the objects have been collected, talk over the difficulties of this example of communication and guidance.

BIBLE READING
Acts 15:36; 16:4-10

RELATIONAL BIBLE STUDY
As always, the questions are designed to encourage people to think about the passage and the topic more carefully. People often wonder if there is a 'right' answer. There isn't! If you and they need reassuring, look at the notes on the passages which reveal how little Luke has seen fit to tell us. The questions take advantage of this scope for differing insights and ideas.

leader's notes

IN DEPTH

MY STORY
Question 1 is an opportunity to 'affirm' and thank the group as a whole for the help they give by sharing themselves and their experiences in these studies. Individual affirmation comes at the next meeting. Question 5 is a chance for people to give themselves or the group a new direction, however small. It may be helpful to explain it with examples, such as: 'I need to ask John (another group member), could you give me a lift to and from work on Tuesday morning because my car will be in the garage?' Receive all the suggestions and responses positively, and then discuss which needs can be met. It might be good first to look at all the ideas which involve the whole group.

GOING FURTHER

Things to remember ...

notes on the Bible verses

 **Acts 15:36, 16:4-10**

15:36 This verse introduces Paul's second missionary journey. Its aim was to repeat the itinerary of the first journey, checking that the new Christians and churches were surviving and growing. But immediately they had to change plan and direction. From other verses, we see that Paul and Barnabas fell out over whether to take Mark with them, and ended up going their separate ways. Eventually, God made good come out of this crisis and Paul later came to be reconciled to Mark.

16:4,5 A second purpose for the journey was to pass on the decisions of the council of apostles and elders which met at Jerusalem (15:1,2). This had met to resolve the question of how far Gentile converts needed to become Jews as well as Christians. The answer, to Paul's relief and to the evident benefit of the Gentile churches, was, in effect, 'not at all'.

16:6-8 We are not told *how* God prevented Paul and his companions from preaching in Asia or entering Bithynia, nor how God revealed his will. The important thing is their reaction to the crisis and the change in their plans – they kept going and pushed every door until the right one opened.

3 Growing through change

CHANGE OF DIRECTION

BIBLE READING
Acts 15:36, 16:4-10

RELATIONAL BIBLE STUDY
1 How do you imagine the Holy Spirit prevented Paul and his fellow travellers from going to Asia or Bithynia? Tick the most appropriate.

a putting up 'No entry' signs
b government restrictions on spreading foreign religions
c their difficulties in speaking the language
d horoscope readings
e a voice from heaven
f visions of Asian and Bithynian men saying 'Go away!'
g human prophecy
h giving them an inner feeling of unease
i other _____

2 When God delays making his will clear, and doesn't 'open doors', what is your reaction? Tick any appropriate responses.

a panic
b pray
c ask for advice
d get depressed
e feel let down
f go round in circles
g put a brave face on it
h feel sure he's keeping something special for me
i other _____

3 I think 'visions' are ... (tick any appropriate answers)

a dreams in your sleep.
b trances while awake.
c pictures while you're praying.
d only for saints.
e very strong hunches.
f imagination.
g a sense of how things ought to be/ what we ought to be doing.
h other _____

IN DEPTH
1 When Paul and his companions reached the point described in 16:6-8, I assume they were ... (tick any that are appropriate)

a sightseeing.
b feeling at a loose end.
c seeing how the Christians were doing.
d delivering the Jerusalem decisions.
e preaching the word.
f praying for guidance.
g other _____

photocopiable response sheet

MY STORY

1 The biggest change of direction in my life has been:

2 The time I was most unsure what God wanted me to do was:

3 The time I felt most clearly guided by God was:

4 Members of this group have strengthened my faith by … (tick any that are appropriate)

a seeing how I'm doing spiritually (see 15:36).
b conveying the teaching of our church leaders (16:4).
c preaching God's word to me (16:6).
d their eagerness to tell the good news to outsiders (16:6-10).
e keeping going despite disappointments (16:6-8).
f answering calls for help (16:9,10).
g discerning God's voice and obeying it (16:10).
h other _____

5 Reflect on 16:9. Are you or the group in a similar position to Paul (needed to give help) or the Macedonian (needing help)?

I think I/we need to say to _____ 'Come over to _____ and help me/ us because

I think _____ is saying to me/ us 'Come over to _____ and help me/ us because

going further

1 Follow Paul's sequence of changes of direction through his second missionary journey, as God turns crises to good effect.

15:37–40	disagreement over Mark outcome – two follow-up journeys, instead of one
16:6–10	closed doors to Asia and Bithynia outcome – recruitment of Luke
16:19–34	Philippian imprisonment outcome – jailer and family become Christians
17	Jewish opposition keeps Paul moving on outcome – three new, strategic churches planted in just a few months

Reflect on the apparent 'disasters' and 'setbacks' in your life. Can you trace any good outcome that God has brought from them?

2 Paul *did* evangelise Asia a short while after his first attempt. He stayed in the capital Ephesus for two and a quarter years (1 Corinthians 16:8,9; Acts 19:8-10). On the other hand, it seems he never visited Bithynia. How can we discern when God is saying 'not yet' to our hopes, ambitions and prayers, and when he is saying 'no'?

4 Growing through change

CHANGE OF SCENE

AIM: to explore how God keeps us moving and growing throughout life, by focusing on 'home' as the heart of our security; and to develop our attitude to moving home (and other changes of role) in response to God's call.

NOTES FOR LEADERS

On the surface, this sessions looks at where we live and how we cope with geographical change. But it also explores the changes of role that we go through at different stages of life. Personal sharing is likely to be deeper than in previous sessions, and the relationships between group members should be deepening to match. Either allow a longer time for some of the sessions, or leave one or two questions out.

PRAYER/ WORSHIP IDEAS

Opening prayer
Read Psalm 23 while asking group members to name in their hearts some of those who are facing changes and who need God's help.

Songs and hymns
The worship for this meeting could helpfully focus on our need to recognise and co-operate with the way the Spirit of God works in us for good, and the constancy of God. Ideas for songs include:

All I once held dear
Create in me a clean heart, O God
Faithful One, so unchanging
Great is thy faithfulness
I give you all the honour
Jesus, you are changing me
Let me have my way among you
When I feel the touch

During the meeting
Ask the group to sketch briefly something which symbolises a change they are facing currently or in the coming months … it might be something literal like a house or a baby, or it might be something symbolic – an altar, a ship, a hand waving goodbye. Share in twos and pray for one another.

ICEBREAKER
Give everyone a photocopied outline map of the British Isles, at least A4 size, and ask them to mark on it all the places where they have lived, with approximate dates. Some people may need to include arrows to other countries. Encourage everyone to talk about their past 'homes' and what they have meant to them. This activity provokes a lot of talking, so, if time is short, people should share in pairs.

BIBLE READING
Acts 18:1-4, 18-21, 24-28; 1 Corinthians 16:19; Romans 16:3-5; 2 Timothy 4:19

RELATIONAL BIBLE STUDY
If yours is a teenage group, look back three or five years, not ten. If anyone has never moved home, they should answer Question 4 in terms of what they think they would like best or least.

IN DEPTH
It may be helpful to ask people to share their answers to Questions 1 and 2 together, as Question 2 goes some way to soothe and cure the painful memories of Question 1. Questions 3 and 4 are both exercises to help affirmation of the group members individually. It is, of course, helpful to ask people to explain *why* they think others are good at x, y or z. You may prefer to work on only one of the questions.

leader's notes

MY STORY
Reassure the group that God continually helps us adjust to new circumstances, however small; and that he gives us Christian friends to help and support us through the growing pains. If they are not sure what area of life God may be calling them to change, suggest they start by looking again at the list in the In Depth section, Question 1. Take seriously any requests for help and prayer from the group and make sure that they are followed up.

GOING FURTHER

notes on the Bible passage

Acts 18:1-4, 18-21, 24-28; 1 Corinthians 16:19; Romans 16:3-5; 2 Timothy 4:19

These passages tell us everything we know about Aquila and Priscilla, one of the New Testament's most widely-travelled couples. Twice in these writings they are 'Aquila and Priscilla', four times 'Priscilla and Aquila'. At the least this suggests there was no automatic 'men first' or 'ladies first' understanding of marriage within the early church. Yet to name the wife first in first-century culture seems so surprising that it is fair to assume that she was more prominent than her husband in one or more respects – maybe in rank or birth, force of personality, teaching gift (Acts 18:26) or authority in the church.

Acts 18:2,3 Emperor Claudius banished all Jews from Rome in AD 49, probably because of the riots they instigated against Christians. We are not told whether Aquila and Priscilla were already Christians, or became so through meeting Paul. *Tentmaker* could be translated more generally as 'leather worker'. Jewish rabbis learned a trade, so that they were not financially dependent on their teaching. Paul continued at times to make a living by his hands, especially when establishing new churches.

Acts 18:18 It's not clear whether Priscilla and Aquila's moves here and later were primarily for business reasons, or as part of Paul's strategy for planting and building new churches. Paul's haircut marked the end of a Nazirite vow (Numbers 6:1–10); Luke does not tell us the reason for the vow.

Acts 18:24-28 When John baptised people he spoke only of repentance and forgiveness. Apollos seems unaware of the coming of the Holy Spirit at Pentecost. Both Priscilla and Aquila lovingly and privately explain this further dimension to the good news; the results in Achaia speak for themselves.

1 Corinthians 16:19 On Paul's return visit to Ephesus, Aquila and Priscilla remember their fellow-Christians in Corinth with warm affection. Their home was being used for fellowship meetings and it is a fair assumption that they were leading that home church.

Romans 16:3-5 About three years later and Priscilla and Aquila are back in Rome, the ban on Jews having been relaxed. They continue to host and possibly lead a church in their home, and Paul counts on them as partners in ministry.

2 Timothy 4:19 Some time later – possibly nearly 20 years on from Paul's first meeting with them – Aquila and Priscilla have returned to Ephesus, and may have reached 'retirement' age.

4 Growing through change

CHANGE OF SCENE

READING
Acts 18:1-4, 18-21, 24-28; 1 Corinthians 16:19; Romans 16:3-5; 2 Timothy 4:19

RELATIONAL BIBLE STUDY
1 List the number of moves that Priscilla and Aquila made in these Bible verses. It will be helpful to know that Paul wrote 1 Corinthians *from* Ephesus, and 2 Timothy *to* Ephesus; and that the verses are given to you in the order in which they were written, each several years apart.

Changes of address for Priscilla and Aquila
_____
_____

2 Whether I'm married or not, the thing I like best about Aquila and Priscilla is that … (put a tick against the most appropriate answer for you right now, and then write '10' against the answer you think you might have given 10 years ago.)

a they work with their hands.
b they are a husband and wife team.
c they are hospitable.
d they have an equal relationship – sometimes 'A and P', sometimes 'P and A'.
e they teach Apollos.
f the church is based in their home.
g they risk their lives for Paul
h there's no slacking off in middle age/retirement.
i they are mobile.
j they are ready for change.
k Other _____

3 I think of 'home' as … (tick the most appropriate)

a where I live now.
b where I lived as a child.
c where my parents live.
d where my belongings are.
e wherever my closest family/ friends are.
f where I can completely relax.
g heaven.
h other _____

IN DEPTH
1 The change of scene I have found hardest so far in my life is … (tick the most appropriate)

a changing school.
b being a teenager.
c leaving home.
d starting college.
e starting work.
f being made redundant.
g being promoted at work.
h breaking up with boyfriend/ girlfriend.
i getting married.
j having children.
k children leaving home.
l middle age.
m death of spouse or someone else close.
n retirement.
o other _____

photocopiable response sheet

2 What's helped me cope with difficult change is … (tick any that are appropriate)

a my family.
b a close friend.
c this group/ another similar group.
d a good cry.
e my Bible.
f a room of my own.

g remembering that Jesus goes through it with me.
h looking forwards, not backwards.
i giving myself a special treat.
j other _____

3 If you were setting sail on a long journey, like Paul, which group members would you take with you in which roles? Put names against the jobs you think they would do best. Your selection doesn't have to be very serious!

captain _____
navigator _____
cook _____
mechanic _____
ship's mascot _____
cabin companion _____

aerobics instructor _____
ship's doctor _____
chief steward _____
look-out _____
entertainer _____
others _____

MY STORY

1 My home is… (tick any that are appropriate)

a my castle.
b home, sweet home.
c a slum.
d for sleep only.
e open house.
f a base for the church.

g my workplace.
h shared with my family.
i not my own.
j other _____
k Think about whether you could complete one or both of these sentences.

a One way God is/may be calling me to change scene/ role is
_____

b One way this group could help me is
_____

going further

1 Use a concordance to research the New Testament's teaching on hospitality. Can you think of any innovative ways to practise it – individually or as a group?

2 *The church that meets at their house.* How far do you think your group to be a church ie an expression of the body of Christ?

3 In Acts 18:26 it appears likely that Priscilla was involved in teaching a man. Does your church have women with teaching gifts and are they able to exercise them?

4 Imagine a typical person in your church. What support does your church give him/her through the changes of life: education/training; friendships; dating; marriage or singleness; having children; coping with teens; mid-life and so on. Are there points at which you feel your church could do more?

5 Growing through change

PRAYER CHANGES THINGS

AIM: to explore and engage in prayer as one of the ways God works through to change us and to achieve his purposes in the world.

NOTES FOR LEADERS
Prayer for healing – the focus of our Bible reading – can be a controversial topic! In the material we shall not go beyond the statements of James 5, but you need to think carefully about whether to introduce either some thoughts of your own or of the church.

PRAYER/WORSHIP IDEAS

Opening prayer
Ask two or three in the group to pray short prayers of thanks to God for his desire to want to communicate with us in many different ways.

Songs and hymns
Our dependence on God and our willingness to be changed by him for his purposes would be useful themes for worship. Songs might include:

Ah Lord God
Here I am, wholly available
It's the presence of your Spirit, Lord, we need
Over the mountains and the sea
Rejoice! Rejoice! Christ is in you
Restore, O Lord, the honour of your name
Spirit of the living God, fall afresh on me
You are my hiding place

During the meeting
Give out some Bibles and get the group to spend a few minutes looking through Psalms. Ask each one to choose an encouraging verse, write it on a piece of paper and pray that verse for the person next to them. Give them the verse to take away.

Closing prayer
Turn into prayers of thanks and challenge any of the statements from the In Depth section which were given substantial agreement by the group.

ICEBREAKER
Give out some slips of paper. Get the group to work in twos. One person has to answer the question: What I would most like to see changed in my church is … The other person has to compose a two-sentence prayer asking God to meet that need. Then swap roles. When everyone has finished, everyone in turn reads out the prayers they have written. If there's time, spend a few minutes discussing the prayer topics. Was there a lot of duplication? Or a lot of variety? Were there any surprises?

BIBLE READING
James 5:13-18

RELATIONAL BIBLE STUDY
Since Questions 3 and 4 ask for honest sharing about discipleship issues, decide whether the sharing should happen in pairs or in the larger group.

IN DEPTH
Question 2 involves a detailed look at two difficult verses and could be omitted or transferred to Going Further if it suits your group and the timing. Question 3 comes closest to linking the subject of prayer in general with the theme of the whole book and could easily take up a lot of time!

MY STORY
This can be a very meaningful experience, depending to some extent on the amount of trust the group members have built up over the time together. It will be helpful if

leader's notes

there is a musician able to accompany unplanned music requests from 2. You may want to modify 3 in the light of your own church's procedure for anointing for healing. Oil is not essential and if it is not a practice of your church you may prefer simply to lay hands on the person wanting healing. If you decide that the whole section is too demanding for your group, substitute Going Further 4.

GOING FURTHER

Things to remember ...

notes on the Bible verses

 **James 5:13-18**

This passage has very much a feel of the body of Christ at work and can really come alive in the setting of a small group of Christians committed to each other.

5:14 The basis of this verse is the tremendous good news that God cares about our health and has the power to restore it. James implies that we should naturally turn to God and his people in times of physical distress. There is nothing 'magic' in the elders or the oil; only God has the power to heal. But there can be great reassurance and support in having the concrete presence of the Christian family in times of need, in hearing them pray, and in feeling their touch as being representative of God's touch.

5:15 There is often no link at all between sin and sickness. But the God-centred believer will want to eliminate the possibility that his illness is in any way a result of his sin. And spiritual healing is always far more vital than physical healing.

5:17,18 James is at pains to stress that Elijah was just as ordinary as we are, yet his prayers were answered in dramatic fashion. The difference between the effectiveness of his prayers and ours may be that Elijah really believed the Word of God – God had promised that idolatry and immorality of the kind that were rife at the time would result in him withdrawing the rain that was needed for a prosperous crop. Perhaps when we know God's word, take God at his word, and have the courage to proclaim God's word, then we might find our prayers are as effective as Elijah's.

5 Growing through change

PRAYER CHANGES THINGS

READING
James 5:13-18

RELATIONAL BIBLE STUDY

1 *The prayer of a righteous man is powerful and effective* (James 5:16) because … (tick any appropriate)

a he's a man.
b he's righteous.
c he prays.
d he prays according to God's will.
e he prays with great faith.
f other _____

2 A righteous person is … (tick any appropriate descriptions)

a anyone who 'does their best' in life.
b any Christian.
c an extra-saintly Christian.
d someone hiding nothing from God.
e someone who no longer sins.
f someone who obeys and pleases God.
g other _____

3 The righteous person's prayers are *powerful* and *effective*. What two words best describe your prayers?
_____

4 I pray… (tick anything appropriate)

a only in emergencies.
b only with others in church or in this group.
c on my own every day.
d twice a day.
e whenever I think about it.
f occasionally.
g all the time.
h other _____

IN DEPTH

1 The reminder that Elijah was a man like us (5:17) encourages us to pray … (tick anything appropriate)

a earnestly.
b for the weather.
c every three and a half years.
d expecting God to do what we pray for.
e expecting God to answer definitely.
f other _____

2 5:15,16 mean that … (tick anything appropriate)

a all sick people will recover if prayed for.
b they will recover if their faith is strong enough.
c they will recover if the faith of those praying is strong enough.
d they will be spiritually cured (ie their sins forgiven), even if not physically.
e they will be totally restored in heaven even if they don't get better in this life.
f other _____

3 Look at the list of statements opposite that people have made about prayer. Alongside each, circle SA (strongly agree), A (agree), NS (not sure), D (disagree) or SD (strongly disagree). Then write a statement of your own about prayer in no more than 10 words.

photocopiable response sheet

Prayer changes things.	SA	A	NS	D	SD
More things are wrought by prayer than this world dreams of.	SA	A	NS	D	SD
Prayer is the most powerful form of energy.	SA	A	NS	D	SD
Satan trembles when he sees the weakest Christian on his knees.	SA	A	NS	D	SD
If you are too busy to pray, you are busier than God intends you to be.	SA	A	NS	D	SD
Prayer is the Christian's vital breath.	SA	A	NS	D	SD
Who rises from prayer a better man, his prayer is answered.	SA	A	NS	D	SD
Prayer changes us because it makes us ready to do God's will.	SA	A	NS	D	SD
Prayer is the nearest approach to God, and the highest enjoyment of him, that we are capable of in this life.	SA	A	NS	D	SD

My own statement about prayer:

MY STORY

Decide which of these four categories from James 5:13-16 best describes you. Write a few words which will help your share your needs/news/requests for a time of praise and prayer as a whole group.

1 in trouble (5:13)/needing prayer

2 happy (5:13)/wanting to share a song of praise (choose a hymn/ song)

3 sick (5:14)/needing prayer and anointing with oil

4 sinner (5:15,16)/wanting to confess and repent

going further

1 What do you understand as the connection between a) sin and sickness and b) prayer, faith and healing? Approach the topics from some other angles.
For *sin and sickness* look up: Deuteronomy 28:58-61; Mark 2:1-12; Luke 13:1-5; John 9:1-3; 1 Corinthians 11:27-32.
For *prayer, faith and healing* look up: Mark 6:1-6; Mark 9:28,29; Luke 8:48,50.

2 Study the Elijah incident in full, in 1 Kings 17 and 18. What does this add to your understanding of the verses from James 5?

3 What do the following passages of teaching about prayer add to James 5? Matthew 18:19,20; Mark 11:24-25; James 1:5-8; 1 John 5:14,15.

4 Pick one or more of these promises as the basis for a time of prayer with the group or on your own in the coming week: Proverbs 15:8, 29; Matthew 7:7-11; Matthew 18:19, 20; Mark 11:24,25; John 14:13, 14; John 16:23,24; Philippians 4:6,7; 1 John 5:14,15.

6 Growing through change

CHANGE AND DECAY?

AIM: to reflect on the changes going on around us in society, and to develop our Christian response to them.

NOTES FOR LEADERS

Although much of the material has been challenging and perhaps daunting to some, try to ensure that the meeting ends on a positive note, with everyone feeling supported and appreciated. Plan to include an opportunity for people to share how they are facing or coping with change differently as a result of the **BODYBUILDERS** course.

This session looks at our political and personal duties to society; in particular, how Christians should react to changes in the law and the moral climate. You will need to exercise enough authority to prevent this from becoming a slanging match! Remind everyone of the generosity of respecting each other's opinions.

PRAYER/ WORSHIP IDEAS

Opening prayer
Ask the group to spend three minutes writing a prayer of two or three sentences of thanks to God for what they have learned about him and his ways during the sessions. Stand in a circle, each one reading out their prayer.

Songs and hymns
Choose songs which affirm the goodness of God and the effectiveness of his people when they are willing to be used by him. Some you could include:

An army of ordinary people
Bind us together
God is good, we sing and shout it
God is working his purpose out
Hallelujah, for the Lord our God
If my people, who are called by my name
Rejoice, rejoice, Christ is in you
We'll sing a new song of glorious triumph

During the meeting
You might also want to pray for each other using the Ice Breaker chart – giving thanks for positive change and praying for areas where change still needs to happen.

Have a few minutes' discussion on the future of the group. Are there plans to do another study? How are people going to keep in touch with one another? Pray about these plans.

Closing prayer
Pray for each one in the group by name using the words of Ephesians 1:15-23.

ICE BREAKER

On a flip chart draw a grid in advance with the numbers 0, 1, 2, 3 along the vertical axis and the following six relationship categories on the horizontal axis:

with God
with family
with the church
with this group
with friends outside the group
with the local community

Ask each person to think about whether their attitude to any of these relationships has changed as they have worked through GROWING THROUGH CHANGE. In a different colour marker pen for each person, mark on the chart the scores they would give themselves for each category:

0 = no change
1 = slight improvement
2 = noticeable progress
3 = big step forward

leader's notes

This is the acid test to see if what's been done in the group has had any real impact on real life! Encourage people not to be over-modest or over-enthusiastic about change, but to be honest and realistic. The final area – that of relationship with the local community – will likely achieve the lowest scores and will lead into this session's theme.

BIBLE READING
Romans 13:1-14

RELATIONAL BIBLE STUDY
Question 2 may cause some problems. You might like to point out that there are two main purposes in considering this: firstly, to make us think about the fact that society is just as bad now as it was in Paul's day, only we probably don't use such strong language about it; and secondly, this question will make some people aware of how few non-Christians they really know. This will help them think more honestly in Question 3 about how involved they actually are in society.

IN DEPTH

MY STORY
You could vary the order of these questions. Obviously the sharing of actual names from Questions 2 is optional, and possibly the information from Question 3, with you deciding as leader how to limit the sharing depending on your knowledge of the group.

GOING FURTHER

notes on the Bible verses

 **Romans 13**

This chapter contains two main perspectives on our duties to society: political (13:1-7) and personal (13:8-14).

13:1–7 Paul's high view of the officials of the Roman Empire is all the more remarkable in that he had suffered injustice at its hands (see Acts 16:19-39), and had witnessed some indifferent policing (Acts 18:12-17). But here he states the principle at stake: God cares about good order in communities, and so establishes the pattern of governments to preserve the peace. Knowingly or not, they are serving God's purpose, so Christians should obey their laws. We may disagree; we may seek to change governments within constitutional rights; but we owe them respect.

13:8–10 We have a never-ending debt to others in society – to love them. Paul spells it out here in its lowest, simplest form: doing them no harm. But the implication of loving our neighbours as ourselves is that we shall do everything we can for their wellbeing.

13:11,12: Paul adds urgency to our duty to care for the rest of society by reminding us that time is short. *Our salvation* in this passage refers to our eventual state of glory in heaven, when Jesus returns.

13:12-14: Paul uses the same image about putting clothes on and off that we looked at in the first session. The flow of his thought here seems to be:

PUT OFF	PUT ON
works of darkness	works of light – living aware of the spiritual battle
immoral behaviour	decent behaviour – living by Jesus' standards
temptations	Jesus Christ – living under his influence

6 Growing through change

CHANGE AND DECAY?

BIBLE READING
Romans 13:1-14

RELATIONAL BIBLE STUDY

1 To me, verses 1-7 sound … (tick any appropriate)

a like common sense.
b very submissive.
c like a mainstream political party manifesto.
d bad news for Christians living under unjust regimes.
e unrealistic.
f the ideal – if everyone was a Christian.
g other _____

2 How much do the people you know go in for the kind of immoral behaviour described in 13:13? Put 0 for not at all, 1 for occasionally, 2 for plenty, 3 for the whole time.

_____ wild parties
_____ getting drunk
_____ sex outside marriage
_____ more extreme sexual activity such as prostitution/ pornography
_____ violent arguments
_____ jealousy

3 Christians down the generations have held wildly different views about how much to be involved with the non-Christian society around them. What do you think? Mark your opinion somewhere on the line.

0	1	2	3	4	5
have as little as possible to do with them, except to convert them to Jesus					get as involved as you can, hoping to change the world for Jesus

IN DEPTH

1 According to 13:1-5, the purpose of governments and rules is to:
_____
_____
_____

How well do you think your current government is doing in keeping the country peaceful and law-abiding? Give them a score out of 10: _____

In Questions 2 and 3 put a cross on the line to represent your opinion:

photocopiable response sheet

2 Taxes (13:6) should be:

| as low as possible, to encourage greater individual initiative | as high as necessary to ensure that everyone gets the benefits they need |

3 Morally, our society seems to be:

| worse than in Paul's times – going down the drain! | about the same as in Paul's time | improved in lots of ways |

4 What are the best ways for Christians to change society for the better? Tick any appropriate.

a preach the good news
b campaign for/ against changes in the law
c get involved at all levels
d pray for it
e form a Christian political party
f other _____

MY STORY

1 Draw a facial expression alongside any that are relevant, to represent their reaction to the fact that you're a Christian:

O partner/girlfriend/boyfriend
O parents
O children
O brother/sister

O boss/teacher
O friends at work/school/college
O your closest friend
O next-door neighbour

2 The person I have the greatest difficulty in loving (13:8) is _____

going further

1 Should 13:1-6 be modified or revised if a country's governing authorities do not acknowledge God or his estimate of right and wrong?

2 How far should churches get involved in political causes and campaigns to change society?

3 Paul wrote in 13:12 about the nearness of God's complete rule. Why are we still waiting?

4 If the day is almost here, why bother with changing society?

'Does your Bible study deal with the issues that friends are talking about at the pub or in the office?'

If you want to talk to your friends about why the Bible is relevant to what they are into, these are the Bible studies for you.
Mike Pilavachi, Soul Survivor

A great way to explore up-to-date issues and concerns in the light of the Bible.
Rev Dr Michael Green, Advisor in Evangelism to the Archbishops of Canterbury and York

How can you engage with friends and colleagues as they discuss best-selling novels, chart music, pop culture TV shows or Oscar-nominated films?

CONNECT can help – innovative, creative and thought-provoking Bible studies for groups available as an electronic download or in print.

Titles available
- Billy Elliot
- The Matrix
- Harry Potter
- TV Game Shows
- Chocolat
- How to be Good
- U2: All that you can't leave behind

With more coming soon

Available from all good Christian bookshops
from www.scriptureunion.org.uk
from Scripture Union Mail Order: PO Box 5148, Milton Keynes MLO, MK2 2YX
Tel 01908 856006
or as an electronic download from www.connectbiblestudies.com

connect Bible Studies are jointly produced by Scripture Union, Premier Media Group and Damaris Trust.